ULTIMATE DANGER ULTIMATE DANGER ULTIMATE

THE ULTIMATE BOOK OF DANGEROUS JOBS

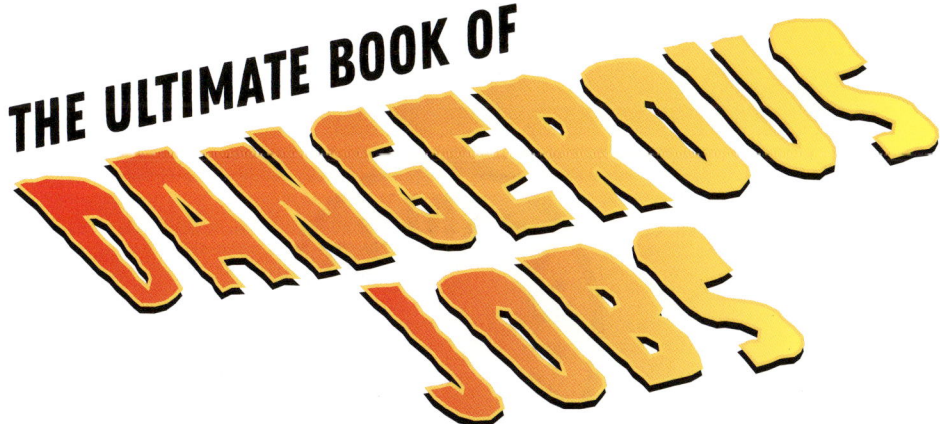

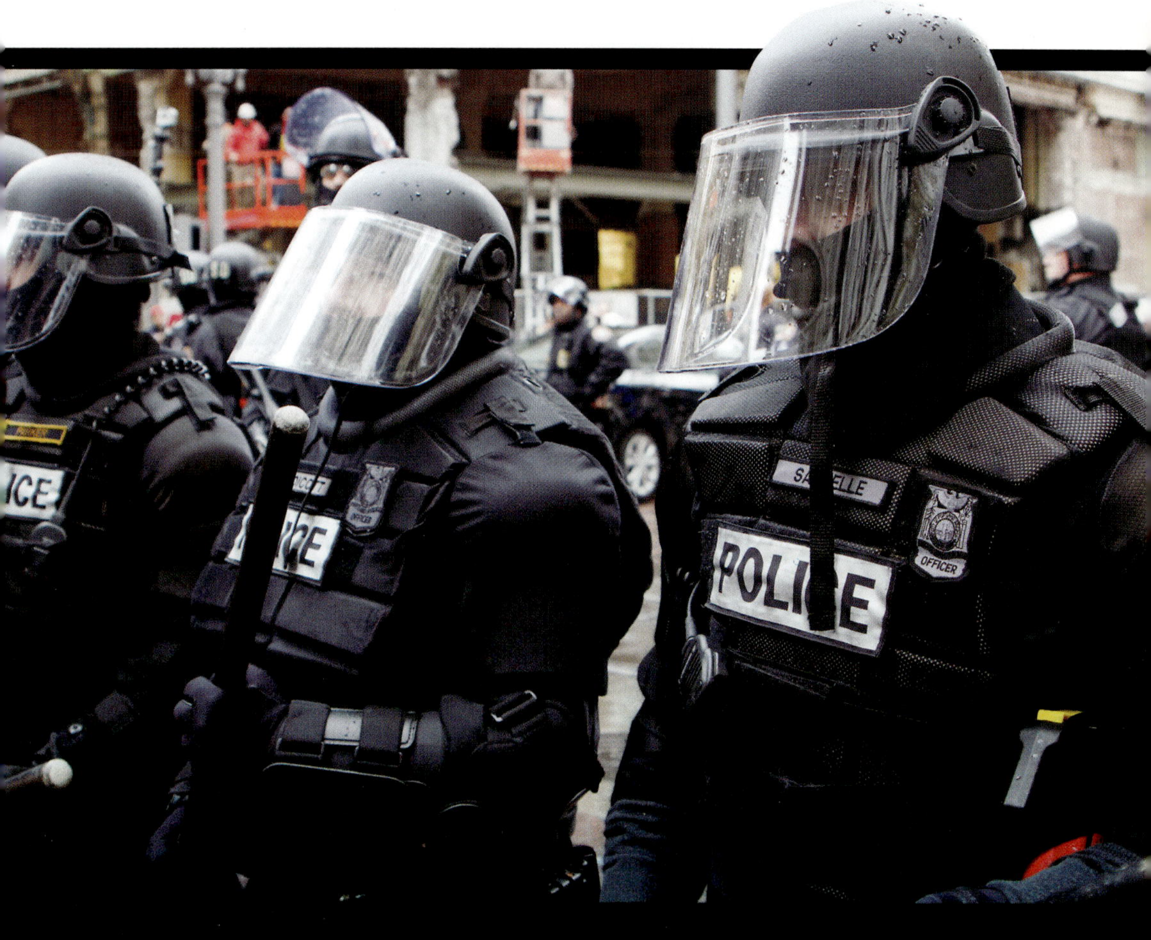

THE ULTIMATE BOOK OF DANGEROUS ANIMALS

THE ULTIMATE BOOK OF DANGEROUS INSECTS

THE ULTIMATE BOOK OF DANGEROUS JOBS

THE ULTIMATE BOOK OF DANGEROUS PLACES

THE ULTIMATE BOOK OF DANGEROUS SPORTS & ACTIVITIES

THE ULTIMATE BOOK OF DANGEROUS WEATHER

THE ULTIMATE BOOK OF
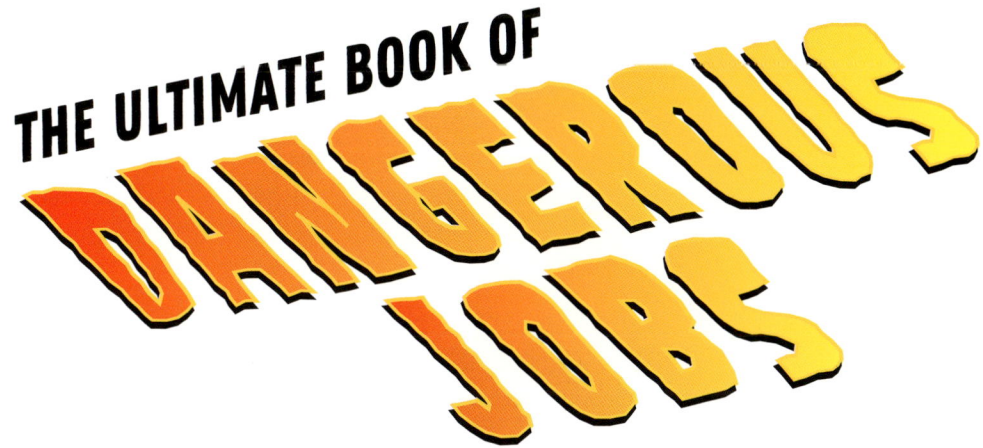

JOHN PERRITANO

MASON CREST
PHILADELPHIA • MIAMI

Mason Crest
450 Parkway Drive, Suite D
Broomall, Pennsylvania 19008
(866) MCP-BOOK (toll-free)
www.masoncrest.com

Copyright © 2020 by Mason Crest, an imprint of National Highlights, Inc. All rights reserved. No part of this publication may be reproduced or transmitted in any form or by any means, electronic or mechanical, including photocopying, recording, taping, or any information storage and retrieval system, without permission from the publisher.

First printing
9 8 7 6 5 4 3 2 1

ISBN (series) 978-1-4222-4224-7
ISBN (hardback) 978-1-4222-4227-8
ISBN (ebook) 978-1-4222-7584-9

Cataloging-in-Publication Data on file with the Library of Congress.

Developed and Produced by National Highlights Inc.
Editor: Peter Jaskowiak
Interior and cover design: Annemarie Redmond
Production: Michelle Luke

QR CODES AND LINKS TO THIRD-PARTY CONTENT

You may gain access to certain third-party content ("Third-Party Sites") by scanning and using the QR Codes that appear in this publication (the "QR Codes"). We do not operate or control in any respect any information, products, or services on such Third-Party Sites linked to by us via the QR Codes included in this publication, and we assume no responsibility for any materials you may access using the QR Codes. Your use of the QR Codes may be subject to terms, limitations, or restrictions set forth in the applicable terms of use or otherwise established by the owners of the Third-Party Sites. Our linking to such Third-Party Sites via the QR Codes does not imply an endorsement or sponsorship of such Third-Party Sites or the information, products, or services offered or accessed through such Third-Party Sites.

CONTENTS

Series Introduction 6

Chapter 1: Dangerous Fun 9

Chapter 2: Protect and Serve 31

Chapter 3: On-the-Job Mayhem 49

Chapter 4: In Service to Country 65

Series Glossary of Key Terms 72

Further Reading and Internet Resources 74

Index 76

Author's Biography and Photo Credits 80

KEY ICONS TO LOOK FOR:

Words to Understand: These words with their easy-to-understand definitions will increase the reader's understanding of the text, while building vocabulary skills.

Sidebars: This boxed material within the main text allows readers to build knowledge, gain insights, explore possibilities, and broaden their perspectives by weaving together additional information to provide realistic and holistic perspectives.

Educational Videos: Readers can view videos by scanning our QR codes, providing them with additional educational content to supplement the text. Examples include news coverage, moments in history, speeches, iconic sports moments, and much more!

Research Projects: Readers are pointed toward areas of further inquiry connected to each chapter. Suggestions are provided for projects that encourage deeper research and analysis.

Series Glossary of Key Terms: This back-of-the-book glossary contains terminology used throughout the series. Words found here increase the reader's ability to read and comprehend higher-level books and articles in this field.

SERIES INTRODUCTION

The *Ultimate Danger* set explores hair-raising hobbies, crime-ridden cities, death-dealing hurricanes, and much more. But what makes something dangerous?

The answer may depend on your perspective. For example, some people would say that guns are so inherently dangerous that having one in the house is unthinkable. But to those who feel comfortable around guns, it's fine to have weapons in the house—even desirable!—as long as they're stored properly. Or consider this: most Americans think of New Zealand as a faraway land with breathtaking scenery and . . . who knows, maybe surfing? The point is, Americans don't know all that much about New Zealand, and it looks adorably harmless to us from so far away. But to New

SOME INFORMATION ON INFORMATION BOXES

Each entry in this set includes an information box that provides basic facts about that topic. Most are self-explanatory, but a few require a little bit of explanation.

In *Dangerous Animals*, one category is called "IUCN Red List." This refers to a database created by the International Union for Conservation of Nature (IUCN). The IUCN assesses the population levels of animal species, and also whether that population is growing or declining. Each species is given a designation, such as "Endangered," "Vulnerable," or, if it's doing well, "Least Concern."

The *Dangerous Places* volume has chapters on dangerous cities and countries—both use population information from the World Population Review website. Almost by definition, the countries and cities covered here tend to be unstable, meaning good data can be difficult to come by. In addition, some countries don't report trustworthy numbers, and movements of refugees can shift population levels rapidly.

In the "Dangerous Countries" chapter, the information box also gives travel advisory information from the U.S. State Department, which assesses the safety (or lack thereof) of countries to help tourists decide whether or not to visit them. Countries are put into four categories, with increasing levels of danger:
- Level 1 (exercise normal precautions)
- Level 2 (exercise increased caution)
- Level 3 (reconsider travel)
- Level 4 (do not travel)

THE ULTIMATE BOOK OF DANGEROUS JOBS

Zealand's indigenous Maori population, who were robbed and oppressed during two hundred years of imperialist rule, New Zealand may not seem quite as adorable.

Given all that, it's clear that "dangerous" is subjective. The term can also be a vaguely insulting one in some contexts. Consider the people of St. Louis, a city frequently included on lists of "most dangerous cities" due to its high rate of violent crimes per citizen. Many residents are annoyed about the city they love ending up on those lists. They'll hold forth passionately about how the statistics are misreported, misunderstood, and just generally unfair.

But not everyone finds "dangerous" to be insulting—for some, the word indicates something that's a heck of a lot of fun. Three of this set's six volumes (*Dangerous Jobs*, *Dangerous Places*, and *Dangerous Sports & Activities*) are partly or entirely devoted to dangers that humans *actively pursue*. Even those of us who would rather not dance with actual danger can't get enough of TV shows and films that scare us, startle us, and let us experience danger at a distance. Some of us even read (and write!) books about the topic. So, without further ado, let's check out the *ultimate* in dangerous creatures, activities, and events.

WORDS TO UNDERSTAND

ACL: acronym for *anterior cruciate ligament,* which is located in the knee
benign: nonthreatening
bona fide: genuine, real
degenerative: wasting away
neurotransmitter: brain chemicals that allow neurons to communicate with one another
perilous: dangerous
prowess: skill, expertise

CHAPTER 1

DANGEROUS FUN

For thousands of athletes across the world, having fun is just part of the job. If you're a sports fan, then you know that playing even the most **benign** sports can sometimes be hazardous. On any given day, athletes are carted off the field because they've injured themselves. Broken bones. Torn ligaments. Concussions. Muscle strains. You name it.

Obviously, certain sports are more dangerous than others. A race car driver, for example, has a better chance of being killed or injured then a professional tennis player—unless, of course, you're on the business end of Serena Williams' serve. A football player is more likely to get injured than a professional bass fisherman. You get the idea.

Every time they practice, train, or compete, athletes are risking life and limb. In fact, according to the U.S. Bureau of Labor Statistics, the risk of injury to professional athletes is 1,000 injuries per 100,000 workers. That puts professional sports in the top five of dangerous occupations.

ALLIGATOR WRESTLER

Dangers: Alligator wrestlers are subject to bites, infections, mauling, and other injuries.

Did You Know? Unlike crocodiles, alligators are native to the United States.

Chris Gillette is a wrestler of the most outrageous kind. He doesn't compete on the wrestling circuit or at the Olympics; instead, his combatants of choice are alligators. Alligators are all over the place in Florida, where Gillette grew up. You can see them on golf courses or in neighborhood parks—just about anywhere, really. He and his wife are two of the world's leading experts on alligators. And while Gillette does not put a gator in a half-nelson choke hold, he enjoys educating the public about these wild and dangerous reptiles.

Let's be clear—wrestling is probably the wrong term to use. There's no head-smacking or arm twisting. Instead, handlers like Gillette coax the animal to open its mouth. Gillette will then try to tuck the creature's head under his chin. He'll also hold the gator's mouth open with his own chin while his arms are outstretched.

Gillette began handling the reptiles to help pay for his college degree in environmental studies. He ended up at the Everglade Alligator Farm, where he entertains the crowd by "wrestling" the beasts. "I've been a professional alligator and crocodile handler for the last decade, and also run tours to safely get people up close to the gators and sharks," he once told a reporter.

NATIVE AMERICANS VERSUS GATORS

Florida is home to thousands of alligators and to a number of attractions where people can "wrestle" with the reptiles. The Seminole and Miccosukee tribes have been wrestling alligators for decades, long before there were roadside attractions. The Miccosukee Indian Village is one of the most famous alligator-wrestling haunts in the state. You can also take an airboat ride through the Everglades or buy all sorts of trinkets at the village.

When he first started wrestling gators, Chris wasn't scared at all. "I loved the rush and excitement of it and didn't even think of the dangers." Once he got older, though, things changed. "I get much more nervous doing shows now as I'm more aware of the dangers involved," he said. "During my show I try to get as close to getting bit without actually getting bitten. It's about balancing the audiences need for excitement with your own need of safety."

Watch this video to see how Chris Gillette "wrestles" an alligator.

Gillette once had a run-in with a gator named Godzilla. The alligator had Chris cornered against the wall. The animal jumped at him and tried to bite his head. "If he had got ahold of me, he'd have caused some serious damage and possibly even killed me." But Godzilla just grazed Gillette's shoulder with his top teeth and left a scar. "That was a pretty hairy moment," Gillette remembered.

An alligator wrestler at work at Everglades National Park, Florida.

DANGEROUS FUN

BASEBALL PLAYER

Dangers: Players are subject to falls, collisions, errant pitches, torn ligaments, strained muscles, and other injuries.

Did You Know? Ty Cobb used to sharpen his baseball spikes so he could injure an opposing player when sliding into a base.

Tony Conigliaro was a hometown Boston boy who made his Major League Baseball (MLB) debut with the Red Sox in 1964 at the age of 19. When Conigliaro got up to the plate for the very first time in Fenway Park, he blasted the first pitch he saw for a home run. During that rookie season, "Tony C" hit 24 dingers, setting a record for the most home runs by a teenager.

Conigliaro's sophomore year was more of the same. He hit 32 home runs, becoming the youngest player to win baseball's home-run crown. By the time he was 22, he'd become the youngest American League player to reach 100 homers. His **prowess** on the ballfield made Conigliaro the most popular athlete in Boston. Not only was he a baseball player, but he was a singer who recorded songs as well. He was also the city's most eligible bachelor.

Then came the pitch. Jack Hamilton had played for many teams in his career, and on the night of August 8, 1967, he was on the mound for the California Angels. It was the fourth inning, and Conigliaro was at bat. Conigliaro crowded the plate, as he always did. Hamilton, known for his wild pitches and spitballs, fired a fastball. Conigliaro wouldn't back off. The ball struck Conigliaro in the face. Fans in the stands and players in the dugout could hear the crunch of the ball meeting Conigliaro's skull. It was a sickening sound. Three of the Red Sox's largest players rushed out to the field and dragged Conigliaro away. "It hurts like hell," Conigliaro said after regaining consciousness. "I thought I was going to die."

Conigliaro lived, but he was never again the same player, underscoring the simple truth that America's pastime can be a dangerous profession when the circumstances conspire against you. According to the University of Southern California, injuries cost the MLB $7 billion in lost wages from 2003 to 2018.

Obviously, not all injuries are as serious as the one that befell Conigliaro, but the number is still staggering. According to one study in the *American Journal of Orthopedics,* from 1998 to 2015, MLB players lost a total of 460,432 days of work because of injuries. That's more than 25,000 a year. The average number of days players spent on the disabled list over the 18 seasons was 55.1. The majority of those hurt suffered shoulder and elbow injuries.

Pitcher Jerome Williams rests on the ground after pulling a hamstring in 2015.

BOXER

Dangers: Head injuries, broken bones, strained muscles, and even death

Did You Know? Mike Tyson once bit off part of Evander Holyfield's ear.

Muhammad Ali is arguably the greatest boxer in the history of the sport, and one of greatest sporting figures of the 20th century. Ali was an Olympic champion, and after he turned professional, he captured the heavyweight title three times, the first athlete to do so. He won 56 bouts in his career, battling some of the sport's most talented and menacing boxers, including Joe Frazier and George Foreman.

In 1984, three years after he retired from boxing, doctors told "The Greatest" that he had Parkinson's disease, a **degenerative**, debilitating malady that kills off the brain cells that produce dopamine, an important **neurotransmitter**. When people lack dopamine, they can have issues with movement. Studies have shown that severe trauma to the brain is a risk factor in developing Parkinson's later in life. It is quite possible boxing ended up killing Ali, who died in 2016 at the age of 72.

No question, boxing is a brutal sport, one in which injury is common, and death lurks in every boxer's corner. In 1980 Ray "Boom Boom" Mancini became the lightweight champion of the world. Mancini defended his title two years later in Las Vegas, Nevada, against a South Korean boxer named Kim Duk-koo.

It was a Saturday, and the fight was broadcast live on CBS. Celebrities were there, along with many others. Mancini should have taken care of Kim easily, but the two duked it out for 14 rounds. In that last round, Mancini pummeled Kim with a left hook. Kim fell backward against the ropes and down to the mat. He never got up, dying in the hospital four days later.

An estimated 500 boxers have died in the ring since 1884, when new rules were introduced. In 2017 researchers in Germany reported that, on average, 10 boxers have died every year since 1900. Eighty percent succumbed to head and neck injuries. In some cases, the boxers died due to epidural hemorrhaging, in which bleeding occurs between the outer membrane of the brain and the skull. Others died of subdural hematomas, in which bleeding occurs in the brain.

Brain damage in boxers doesn't necessarily lead to immediate death, but the Grim Reaper can still show up later in life. In addition, permanent brain damage can lead to a number of additional health problems.

Muhammad Ali (left) fights Leon Spinks in February 1978.

FOOTBALL PLAYER

Dangers: Falls, collisions, concussions, broken bones, paralysis, and other injuries plague football players.

Did You Know? The career of New York Giant Turk Edwards ended in 1940 after he blew out a knee as he walked back to the sidelines after the coin toss.

Like the gladiators of ancient Rome, today's professional football players are extremely hard workers who pound one another for the crowd's enjoyment. On-the-job injuries have always been a big part of the game, and players expect to be hurt. But nothing could have prepared Rashad Johnson for the injury he suffered. In 2013, Johnson, a defensive back for the Arizona Cardinals, started one game with 10 fingers and finished it with 9 ½.

The Cardinals were playing the New Orleans Saints that day when Johnson ran back a punt. He was driven into the artificial turf. When he walked back to the sidelines, Johnson took off his glove. What he saw shocked him and everyone else—the top of his middle finger was severed just above the knuckle. It was an unexpected and bloody mess. How the injury occurred, no one seemed to know, not even Johnson. Doctors eventually shaved the bone down and stitched up the wound. Johnson was back on the field two games later.

Joe Theismann wasn't as lucky. Theismann was the Washington Redskin's quarterback when Lawrence Taylor tackled him in 1985, breaking his leg in several places. The hit ended Theismann's career. People all around the world watched in horror as Theismann's leg bone protruded from his skin, highlighting just how brutal professional football can be.

REST IN PEACE

While football can be a brutal game, only one NFL player has died on the field. His name was Charles Frederick "Chuck" Hughes, and he played from 1967 to 1971. He died of a massive heart attack against the Chicago Bears.

Tackling in football can take a toll on the body over time.

Broken bones, torn ligaments, strained muscles, and blown-out knees are common in professional football, as are concussions, which can hobble a player for years after he leaves the game. In 2017 the National Football League (NFL) released data on the league's injury rate. It showed a 13.5 percent increase in diagnosed concussions from the previous season. Ninety-one players suffered concussions during preseason practice and games, up from 71 the year before. Consider some of these other numbers:

- On average, there were 6.9 injuries reported during Thursday night games in 2017—a 1.6 percent increase over the previous season.
- In 2017 there were 57 **ACL** tears among players during the preseason, regular season, and postseason. ACL is short for *anterior cruciate ligament*, which stabilizes the knee joint.
- During that same period there were 151 tears of the knee's medial collateral ligament, up from 144 in 2016.

GYMNAST, ACROBAT

Dangers: Falls, broken bones, torn muscles, and strained ligaments are common injuries, and death is a risk for some acrobats and circus performers.

Did You Know? Aspiring acrobats often attend a formal circus school to hone their gymnastic abilities.

Wrist fractures, ACL tears, broken legs, torn muscles . . . the list of injuries is seemingly endless whenever gymnastics is involved. While many gymnasts compete as amateurs, others tumble, spin, and twirl professionally, many under the tent of the circus big top. And sometimes, those **perilous** moves can turn deadly.

In 2014 a "human chandelier" made of eight acrobats came plummeting to the ground during a performance in Providence, Rhode Island. The performers, hanging from their hair, were suspended two stories up. As they were doing their routine, something went wrong, and the chandelier collapsed. Eight of the gymnasts suffered non-life-threatening injuries.

Four years later, Yann Arnaud, an acrobat for the Cirque du Soleil, fell to his death during a performance in Tampa, Florida. Working with a partner, Arnaud was spinning high above the stage as he gripped the straps of a rope. The pair of acrobats then separated, flying off in different directions above the crowd. Arnaud lost his grip and fell to his death.

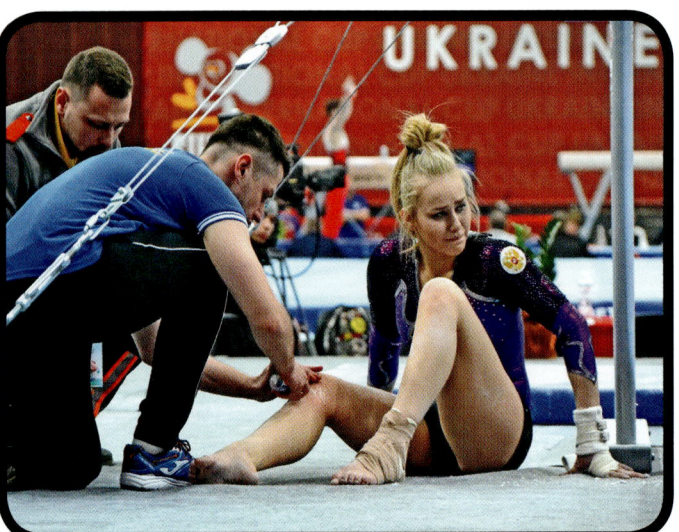

The Russian gymnast Alla Sosnitskaya is looked at by doctors after injuring herself in 2018.

THE ULTIMATE BOOK OF DANGEROUS JOBS

HOCKEY PLAYER

Dangers: Playing hockey can result in falls, collisions, knocked-out teeth, concussions, cuts, bruises, and more serious injuries.

Did You Know? In 1959, Jacques Plante of the Montreal Canadiens was the first hockey goalie to wear a mask.

Danger on the rink may come from flying pucks or swinging sticks . . . or from other players!

Have you ever seen a hockey player smile? There's a decent chance that he or she was missing some teeth. Hockey players are constantly getting checked, tripped, slashed, and pummeled as they zip around the ice at more than 37 miles per hour (59.5 kmh). In the old days, players did not wear helmets or protective pads. Goaltenders didn't even wear masks! These days, all players wear defensive gear. Still, concussions, torn muscles, and other injuries occur.

One of the most gruesome accidents occurred on March 22, 1989. On that day, Clint Malarchuk, a goalie for the Buffalo Sabres, was doing what all goalies do—guarding the net. The Sabres were playing the St. Louis Blues that night, when two of the opposing players crashed into Malarchuk. As they collided, the skate of one of the players slashed the artery in Malarchuk's neck, spewing blood across the ice. He almost bled to death, and some fans fainted.

A 2014 study by the St. Michael's Hospital in Toronto and the University of Toronto found that National Hockey League teams and their insurance companies paid about $683 million in salary to injured players during the previous three seasons. In 2015 researchers published the results of a seven-year injury study in which they looked at players who participated in international tournaments. They found an injury rate of 14.2 per 1,000 player-games.

JOCKEY

Dangers: Jockeys are prone to falls and collisions, of course, and these can lead to serious injury or death.

Did You Know? In 2016, a four-horse collision sent two jockeys to the hospital. The horses were not injured.

Jose Flores was an experienced jockey, winning 4,650 thoroughbred races during his storied three-decade career. He also earned a ton of money—more than $64 million. But Flores died in 2018 when the horse he was riding fell, throwing Flores headfirst into the turf.

Horse racing is very popular, yet it is also one of the most hazardous occupations. Jockeys, not to mention horses, risk death every time they race. Thoroughbred horses can run up to 40 mph (60 kmh). Horses can fall. Jockeys can tumble. In the 1990s, the American Medical Association looked at the injury rate among jockeys. Of 6,545 injuries tabulated between 1993 and 1996, 20 percent were head injuries, more than 15 percent were leg injuries, and nearly 11 percent were back injuries.

In 2013 researchers studied the injury rate for thoroughbred and quarter horse jockeys in California. Running the numbers from 2007 to 2011, the scientists concluded that a licensed thoroughbred jockey in California can expect to fall off his mount and be injured every 502 rides, while quarter horse riders can expect to have a fall every 318 rides.

Horse racing at Bush Hill in Barbados, West Indies

LION TAMER

Dangers: Mauling, severe bites and cuts, death

Did You Know? Irina Bugrimova was the first female lion tamer in the Soviet Union. She was mauled by lions on multiple occasions, but always went on with the show.

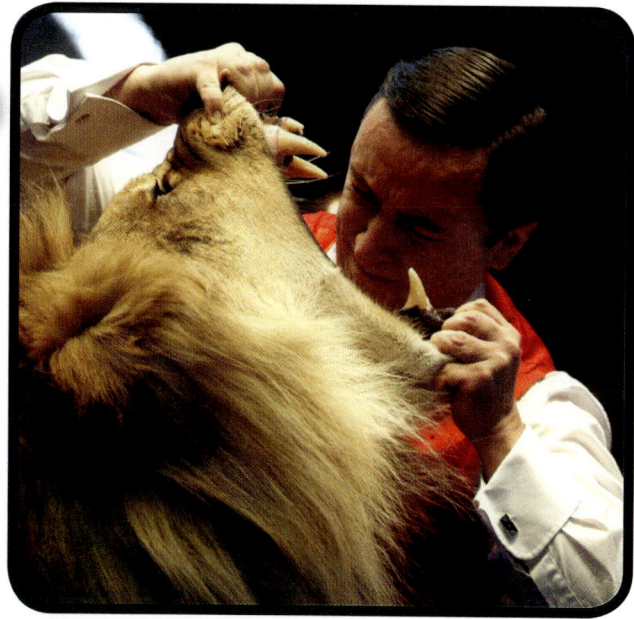

A lion tamer at the Moscow Circus risks his head in the lion's mouth.

The French circus performer Henri Martin captivated crowds in 1819 when he entered a tiger's cage and emerged unscathed. He eventually began incorporating lions in his act, becoming the first **bona fide** lion tamer.

Lion tamers (they like to be called "trainers") have been the staple of circuses ever since. Female and male tamers often dress in fancy costumes, directing their feline partners to do a variety of tricks—many times to the lions' chagrin. In the 1920s, Clyde Beatty used a pistol and whip to keep his cats in check.

Even the most experienced lion tamers can get injured, or worse. That's what happened to Islam Shaheen, 35, who had been performing with the big cats for a decade. Shaheen was in Egypt in 2016 when a group of lions pounced on him in the cage, ripping his neck and pinning him to the ground. Shaheen suffered a fractured skull, cuts to his face and neck, and abdominal bleeding, among other wounds. He died in the hospital days later.

MATADOR

Dangers: Goring, trampling, death

Did You Know?
Francisco Romero reportedly invented the bullfighter's *muleta*, or red cape.

The writer Ernest Hemingway was enthralled with bullfighting. He once wrote, "Bullfighting is the only art in which the artist is in danger of death." Many would take exception to Hemingway's depiction of bullfighting, since it's the bull, more often than not, that ends up dead.

Still, some fans liken bullfighting to dancing, where the grace and skill of the matador transcends the cloud of danger that hangs over the arena.

While bullfighting takes on many different forms in different cultures, the best known is the Spanish style. In Spanish bullfighting, the matador enters the ring during a parade called the *paseíllo*. Next, the bull trots in with great fanfare and trumpets sounding. Before the matador gets to work, however, his assistants ride in on armored horses. They are the *picadors*, who attack the bull with lances, striking it where the shoulders and neck come together. As they do, the matador watches and learns. He tries to understand how the bull is going to react.

The prodding also weakens the bull's neck. The animal slumps its shoulders and head so that the matador can go in for the kill when the time is right. The matador taunts the beast with a cape called the *capote de brega*. The matador swings his cape, causing the bull to charge. If the matador does his job right, he'll expertly maneuver himself out of the way several times, before focusing on the kill.

During the last charge, the matador will thrust his sword into the bull's neck, between the shoulder blades and into the heart. If everything goes as planned, the bull will die.

Matadors are well paid, making up to $100,000 a fight. In 2017 Iván Fandiño, a celebrated matador, was killed in France after being gored in the chest. The bull's horn had plunged deep into his lungs. As he was taken from the arena, Fandiño could be heard yelling "hurry up, I am dying."

A matador at work in Moita, Portugal, in 2016.

DANGEROUS FUN

RACE CAR DRIVER

Dangers: Motorsport racing has many dangers, including collisions, crashes, broken bones, internal injuries, head injuries, and death.

Did You Know? During a Sportsman race at Daytona International Speedway in 1960, 37 out of 68 cars were involved in a collision, the largest ever for the sport. Luckily, no one died.

Dale Earnhardt Sr. was a stock car legend, the king of the NASCAR circuit and a 7-time Winston Cup champion with a total of 76 victories. At the Daytona 500 in 2001, Earnhardt was on the last lap, traveling at 180 miles (290 km) per hour. Sterling Marlin was close behind. Marlin was Earnhardt's longtime friend, a bond forged by competition and respect. Earnhardt was running in the middle, racing for third and protecting the lead of teammate Michael Waltrip. Earnhardt moved to the left to block, touching Marlin's right-front bumper. In that instant, Earnhardt's black No. 3 Chevy spun out of control and moved up the track in front of Ken Schrader's car.

Earnhardt's car hit the wall nearly head-on as Schrader's car pushed it. When both vehicles came to a stop, Schrader rushed out and looked inside Earnhardt's car. Schrader immediately called for paramedics. The race had ended. Waltrip had won, and Earnhardt was gravely injured. It took NASCAR officials three hours to make the announcement that he had died.

Earnhardt's death was a wake-up call to all race car drivers. Motorsports are often exhilarating and exciting, regardless of whether it is Formula 1, NASCAR, Grand Prix, or another type of race. While engineers have designed cars and

SAFETY FIRST

One of the most important safety improvements in motorsport racing is the HANS device, which supports the head and neck. It is a collar made of carbon fiber and Kevlar, a synthetic substance often used in bulletproof vests. It prevents a driver's head from snapping forward or to the side during a wreck.

THE ULTIMATE BOOK OF DANGEROUS JOBS

CHECK IT OUT!

Create a poster showing all the different types of equipment that NASCAR drivers use to protect themselves from getting injured.

equipment to keep racers as safe as possible, motorsports is still one of the most dangerous sports in the world. Twenty-eight NASCAR drivers have died since 1959. Hundreds of other racers around the world have died over the decades in various other races. It's almost too many to count.

Yet death isn't the only thing that makes motorsport racing dangerous. Crashes abound in racing, injuring many drivers. Some suffer blunt force trauma, which can result in broken bones and soft tissue injuries. When Dan Wheldon was the reigning Indy 500 champion in 2001, he crashed during the 11th lap at the Las Vegas Motor Speedway on October 11. It was a 15-car accident. Wheldon's car flew 325 feet (99 m) into the fence. He died of blunt force trauma to the head.

Sometimes racers are injured from penetrating wounds, which occur when a projectile or stationary object rips through the body. Racers can also suffer spinal cord injuries, head injuries, and injuries to internal organs when a car rapidly decelerates.

In Talladega, Alabama, driver Carl Edwards goes flying after getting hit in 2009.

DANGEROUS FUN 25

RODEO CLOWN

Dangers: Rodeo clowns suffer from falls, broken bones, torn ligaments, concussions, and other injuries.

Did You Know? Competitive rodeo began in the early 1900s.

Being a rodeo clown is not all fun and games. In fact, the job is deadly serious. This is a high-risk occupation that has the specter of death hanging over every clown who steps into the rodeo arena.

First, a bit of history. Back in the day, rodeo clowns were just that—clowns. They entertained spectators between rodeo events. Over time, however, the rodeo clown's job grew. Along with "barrel men," rodeo clowns began to protect cowboys from serious injury during professional bull-riding competitions. When a cowboy is thrown from a bull or jumps off, rodeo clowns spring into action so the cowboy can run to safety. Barrel men, by contrast, maneuver a barrel around the arena in case a cowboy has to duck for cover.

Underneath the makeup, baggy pants, and Stetson hat, rodeo clowns don protective equipment that keeps them from getting injured. One professional rodeo clown once said that facing a charging bull was like staring down a car taking aim at him at 20 miles an hour (32 kmh). He also said that during his career, he has suffered 24 broken bones, three concussions, a dislocated jaw, and various internal injuries. Oh, yeah . . . there was also that time he had an ear torn off.

Rodeo clowns (in the colorful outfits) race in to protect a rider who's fallen off his bull at the 2017 Professional Bull Riders World Finals in Las Vegas, Nevada.

RUGBY PLAYER

Dangers: Falls, collisions, crashes, broken bones, death, internal injuries, head injuries.

Did You Know? Rugby players are injured three times more than soccer players.

Battling for the ball at the World Rugby Nations Cup in 2016.

There's no doubt about it: American football players are tough. But rugby players might just be tougher. They can take as much, if not more, punishment than any NFL linebacker. According to one estimate, 25 percent of rugby players are injured each season. Spinal injuries top the list.

Rugby is a fast-moving, bone-crushing sport—similar to football, but more intense. While football players wear helmets and other protective gear, rugby players wear nothing but shirts, cleats, socks, and shorts.

A tackle on the rugby field can lead to death. In August 2018, World Rugby player Louis Fajfrowski was killed after an opponent tackled him. Although Fajfrowski left the field under his own power, he later vomited and passed out, before dying in the dressing room. According to the journalist Mark Reason, 11 rugby union or rugby league players died of head injuries between 2013 and 2017.

As in American football, concussions are a big problem in rugby. The situation became noticeable to the public when several top-name rugby players revealed their struggles with head injuries. The brains of other pro rugby players have been analyzed after their deaths, and pathologists have confirmed they suffered from CTE, or chronic traumatic encephalopathy. CTE is a brain condition caused by repeated blows to the head. It is associated with dementia.

SNAKE CHARMER

Dangers: Bites from poisonous snakes can lead to illness or death.

Did You Know? Many snake charmers remove the fangs from their snakes, meaning the practice is much more dangerous for the snakes (who can die of infection after surgery).

A snake charmer in Kerala, South India.

Take a stroll through any Indian market or festival, and you're likely to see a snake charmer. Snake charmers practice the ancient art of hypnotizing a poisonous snake, supposedly by playing an instrument.

Snake charming is an age-old tradition that some believe had its beginnings in ancient Egypt. The tradition is slowly dying out, however, mainly because India passed a law more than 40 years ago banning ownership of serpents. Nonetheless, many snake charmers still practice their craft in India and other parts of Southeast Asia, as well as in the Middle East and North Africa. They move from place to place, holding their serpents in a basket suspended from bamboo poles.

When it is showtime, the charmer sits cross-legged on the ground in front of the closed basket. As he removes the top of the basket, he begins playing a tune from a flute-like instrument, generally sculpted from a gourd. The snake—most of the time, a cobra—seems to be drawn to the tune, uncurling its body from the basket. But snakes have no external ears and can't really hear the music. The real reason they rise up is because they feel threatened by the charmer.

The snake seems mesmerized, as if it under some type of spell. Some charmers will kiss the snake on its face or hold it by the tail and gently swing it back and forth. Some will even dare the audience to touch the snake. It is a dangerous way to make a living, as one well-placed bite can kill the charmer.

SNAKE MILKERS

Dangers: Bites from poisonous snakes can lead to illness or death.

Did You Know? One gram of snake venom can sell for about $2,000.

You can milk a cow. You can milk a goat. But did you know you can also milk a snake? There are nearly 3,000 snake species in the world. Of that number, around 400 or so are venomous. While some people see danger anytime they glimpse one of these slithering reptiles, others see dollar signs. Snake milkers "milk" snakes for their venom. It's literally a hands-on job, and one slip can be fatal.

Scientists need snake venom for a variety of reasons. Most importantly, they use it in medicines and as an antivenom potion. The idea is if a person gets bitten by a snake, the antivenom can make them well again—if they get to the hospital in time. Snake venom can also be used to help patients who have malignant cancerous tumors or who have suffered a stroke.

The snake milker will pick a snake from its cage and stretch latex, a thin rubbery covering, over a jar. The snake bites the jar, and the milker extracts the venom by massaging the reptile's venom glands, or by applying an electric current that contracts the snake's muscles. Either way, the venom spills into the jar. It is then freeze-dried and shipped to drug companies, laboratories, and research universities. On average, snake milkers make around $2,500 a month.

DANGEROUS FUN 29

WORDS TO UNDERSTAND

demilitarized zone: an area between warring countries that is devoid of military installations, based on treaties or other agreements
fire suppressant: a chemical that can extinguish a fire
jurisdiction: the power to make legal decisions and judgments
ordnance: military explosives, such as missiles and bombs
pathogen: bacterium, virus, or other microorganism that causes disease

THE ULTIMATE BOOK OF DANGEROUS JOBS

CHAPTER 2

PROTECT AND SERVE

When someone calls 911 in an emergency, there are people who will risk life and limb to respond. Some are police; others are firefighters. Once they leave for work, most never know whether they will return at day's end. It is often a mystery as to what awaits them on the other end of that 911 call.

The dangers these first responders and others face are many. A minor traffic accident can turn into a deadly gun battle. A small house fire can morph into a raging inferno. A suspicious package can be a bomb ready to go off. Those who run into danger instead of away from it are a unique breed.

Some put their lives on the line for other reasons. Astronauts, for example, do so to further the aims of science, exploration, and society writ large. Scientists risk becoming ill to stop diseases from spreading. These are not easy jobs. The dangers are immediate, and the achievements often go unrecognized, because it's difficult for the public to appreciate problems that never occur, such as *not* developing a disease they weren't aware of in the first place.

ASTRONAUT

Dangers:
Astronauts face many risks, including fire, suffocation, crashes, and explosions.

Did You Know? The first woman in space was a Soviet cosmonaut, Valentina Tereshkova, who blasted off on June 16, 1963.

It was 1967, and the United States and the former Soviet Union were locked in an intense race to the Moon. On January 27, 1967, three U.S. astronauts, Gus Grissom, Edward White II, and Roger Chaffee, all crew members of Apollo I, were training for an upcoming mission. They were enclosed in a space capsule sitting on top of a Saturn 1B rocket. Without warning, an electrical system in the capsule sparked, creating a deadly inferno inside the spacecraft. The three astronauts suffocated as smoke quickly filled the cabin. In that instant, Grissom, White, and Chaffee became the first casualties of the U.S. space program. Since the early days of space flight in the 1960s, 18 astronauts, including several Soviet cosmonauts, have died during various space missions.

Anything can happen during space travel, including mechanical problems, system failures,

and human error. One of the worst tragedies occurred in 1986, when the space shuttle *Challenger* exploded 73 seconds after takeoff from the Kennedy Space Center in Florida. All seven crew members, including a teacher named Christa McAuliffe, died.

In addition to defying death in space, the bodies and minds of astronauts can undergo serious changes. For one thing, space can be a lonely place, as astronauts are often away from families and friends for long periods. Such isolation can cause a variety of mental health issues. Space is also dangerous, in and of itself. Astronauts are exposed to radiation. Since there is no gravity in space, astronauts are required to exercise every day to keep their muscles and bones healthy. These are just a few of the endless problems astronauts face.

Bruce McCandless takes a spacewalk outside the space shuttle *Challenger* in 1984.

PROTECT AND SERVE

BOMB SQUAD TECHNICIAN

Dangers: Death, dismemberment, and other trauma are always possible on this job.

Did You Know?
The first bomb squad was led by Sir Thomas Knyvett, who stopped Guy Fawkes from blowing up Britain's House or Lords in 1606.

The packages came in the mail in yellow envelopes. All were suspicious. Someone had sent them to CNN, the cable news network. Others were addressed to former president Barack Obama, former U.S. secretary of state Hillary Clinton, and former vice president Joe Biden, among others. In that perilous moment in the fall of 2018, the bomb squad was called into action. No one knew what was in the packages—that was a job better left to the experts.

As it turned out, the envelopes contained explosive devices—simple pipe bombs made by a man in Florida. The bombs never went off, and no one was injured, but the bomb squad technicians who responded were ready to protect the public.

As long as there have been people building bombs, there have been people trained to defuse and dispose of them. Generally, you never hear of the bomb squad until it is called into action. Yet bomb squad technicians are always training, always trying to keep one or two steps ahead of bomb-makers. The techs usually come into contact with two main types of explosives: **ordnance** bombs and improvised explosive devices (IEDs). Ordnance bombs are explosives built for military use and are made in factories. Bombs made by individuals such as the Florida man who sent the bombs in 2018 are IEDs.

Most bomb-hunting and disposal activities fall under the **jurisdiction** of local bomb squads. For example, the New York City Police Department's bomb squad responded to CNN's offices in Manhattan when the packages arrived. The military has its own bomb technicians to search for and clear ordnance from military facilities, including gun and bomb ranges.

In addition to diffusing and disposing of bombs, bomb squads conduct investigations. Most techs train at the Federal Bureau of Investigation's Hazardous

Devices School at the Redstone Arsenal in Alabama. The FBI also has its own bomb squad that travels the world investigating explosive-related activities.

Bomb techs are part cop, part scientist. They might blow a door open so police can storm into a building. They might help clear a dangerous drug lab. They might respond to a bomb inside a vehicle. They deal with everything; from simple pipe bombs made by teenagers to sophisticated bombs made by terrorists.

A bomb disposal expert approaches a suspicious device during a training exercise in Colchester, England.

EMERGENCY MEDICAL TECHNICIAN, PARAMEDIC

Dangers: EMTs and paramedics face many dangers, including bites, infections, car accidents, toxic exposure, and muscle strains and pulls.

Did You Know? Spain was the first country to use ambulances, in 1487.

On May 19, 2018, the radios of emergency medical service providers across the United States went silent at the same time. This was not a technical glitch, but a moment of silence for emergency medical technicians (EMTs) and paramedics who have died in the line of duty.

You might not think that being an EMT is a dangerous job. But one study suggests that the death rate for emergency medical service (EMS) workers is 13 per year, or 7.0 per 100,000 full-time workers, a high number compared to other occupations. Moreover, according to the Centers for Disease Control and Prevention (CDC), 22,000 EMS workers visit the emergency room each year for injuries sustained while on the job. The most common are strained backs and necks, which occur while responding to 911 calls. About 6,000 EMS personnel, the CDC says, are also exposed to harmful substances, including bodily fluids of their patients.

Every time an EMT or paramedic responds to a call, they are navigating a perilous world. Most EMT deaths are the result of highway crashes, while others involve cars and other vehicles striking EMS workers. Other workers have died during aerial transports of patients.

Paramedics climb up a mountain to reach the victims of a helicopter crash in Mallorca, Spain.

EPIDEMIOLOGIST

Dangers:
Epidemiologists come into contact with dangerous diseases, putting them at risk.

Did You Know?
Dr. Janet Elizabeth Lane-Claypon was one of the founders of epidemiology.

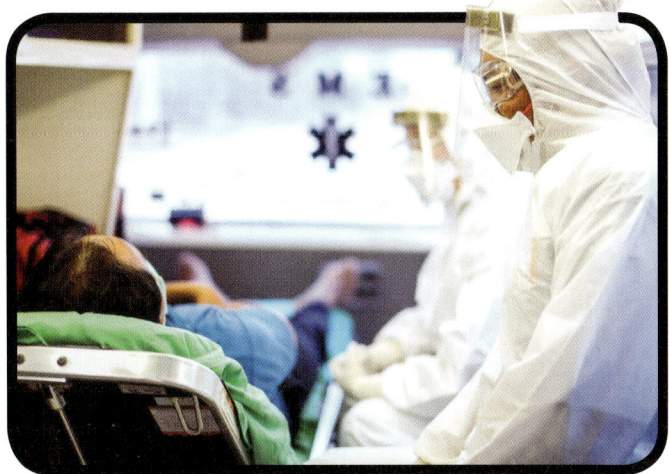

The disease called Ebola is extremely contagious, so doctors who work with Ebola patients must wear elaborate protective gear to keep themselves safe.

Epidemiologists are not only scientists and doctors: they are also disease detectives, dispatched around the world whenever there is a deadly outbreak. Like all good detectives, they look for clues, asking various questions: Who is sick? What are their symptoms? When did they become ill? Where might they have been exposed to the disease?

The goal of the epidemiologist is to stop, or at the very least slow down, outbreaks of **pathogens** that cause Ebola, salmonella, anthrax, influenza, and other diseases. They'll respond to both natural disasters and terrorist attacks. But in the course of their work, the scientists put themselves at risk, as they are constantly coming into contact with disease.

The suspects they look for are among the deadliest on the planet. To that end, epidemiologists have an entire wardrobe to keep themselves safe. They put respirators over their mouths and noses to keep from breathing in dangerous pathogens. They'll don protective gowns, gloves, and facial shields. They'll also use equipment to help them reach remote locations, such as traps to catch disease-carrying bats, some of which can cause serious illnesses in humans.

PROTECT AND SERVE

FIREFIGHTER

Dangers: Fighting fires is difficult work, and firefighters suffer broken bones, severe burns, smoke inhalation, and strained muscles, as well as facing death in many instances.

Did You Know? Boston established the first fire department in America, in 1679.

Texas City, Texas. April 16, 1947. Workers are loading fertilizer onto a freighter docked in Galveston Bay. The fertilizer, ammonium nitrate, is extremely combustible. The U.S. Army used it during World War II, which had ended two years earlier. Along with the fertilizer, workers load the freighter, *Grandcamp*, with tobacco and ammunition. As the longshoremen go about their jobs, someone spots smoke billowing out of one of the ship's holds. The call goes out. Teams of firefighters arrive, sirens wailing and lights blaring. They grab hoses. They grab fire extinguishers. But it is not enough.

There are 2,300 tons (2,086 metric tons) of cargo in the *Grandcamp*. As firefighters pour water and **fire suppressant** on the burning freight, workers frantically try to off-load the ammunition. When the clock strikes 9 a.m., flames pour out of the hold. Minutes later, the ship explodes. The blast is so powerful that it lifts another ship out of the water and propels the *Grandcamp*'s massive anchor 2 miles (3.22 km) from the ship. When the fire is finally put out, 581 people lay dead, including 27 firefighters—making this one of the worst fire-related disasters in U.S. history.

Firefighters respond to a litany of emergencies, including fires, car accidents, and search-and-rescue operations. From 1990 to 2004, according to the U.S. Federal Emergency Management Agency (FEMA), there were, on average, 129 firefighting

CHECK IT OUT!

Research the history of firefighting or policing in the United States and create a visual timeline of major milestones. The timeline can take the form of a slide show, a poster, or a video.

fatalities in the United States every year—or 117, if we don't include those who died during the September 11, 2001, terrorist attack on the World Trade Center in New York City. From 2004 to 2016, FEMA reports, there was an annual average of 102 firefighting deaths. In 2018, the fatal injury rate was 6.1 for every 100,000 workers.

Not all of these on-duty deaths occurred as firefighters battled blazes, however. Some died during training exercises; others while responding to other emergencies. Some firefighters died because of heart attacks, others because they were trapped in burning buildings or battling wildfires. In 2016, 60 percent of firefighter deaths occurred during non-emergency situations, such as training and other activities, while the remainder occurred during emergency situations.

LANDMINE REMOVER

Dangers: Deadly explosions

Did You Know?
During World War II (1939–1945), German soldiers buried a type of mine the Americans called "Bouncing Betty." Once the foot of a soldier stepped on it, the mine would bounce up around 3 feet (1m) and explode.

In 1950, Communist North Korea invaded the South, sparking the Korean War. Their armies fought battles in many places. During the conflict, soldiers buried landmines designed to maim and kill. Although the Korean War ended in an armistice agreement in 1953, thousands of landmines littered the peninsula, specifically the DMZ, the **demilitarized zone** between both countries. In 2018, with tensions between both sides easing, the two Koreas started to remove the mines in the DMZ.

Korea isn't the only place where landmines continue to pose problems. Once they are in the ground, a landmine doesn't care whom it hurts. Around 50 countries have active programs to remove landmines. One small slipup can kill. In 2016 an Australian landmine remover was killed in Iraq as he tried to defuse a landmine placed by militants of the Islamic State.

Much of the work is done by civilians, although they are generally trained by soldiers. Some devices they remove date back to World War I (1914–1918), while others were buried more recently. By one estimate, there are 110 million landmines buried all over the world. One person is killed by a landmine every 15 minutes.

A sign in Cambodia warns of the danger of landmines in the area.

LIFEGUARD

Dangers: Lifeguards risk drowning and hypothermia, as well as other injuries.

Did You Know? U.S. president Ronald Reagan was once a lifeguard in Illinois. He saved 77 lives.

Lifeguard on duty on Australia's Gold Coast.

In 2014 Ben Carlson, a lifeguard in Newport Beach, California, jumped into the ocean to save a struggling swimmer. Carlson, who was 32 at the time, had 15 years of experience when he dived from a rescue boat into the water. First he threw the swimmer a buoy, and then raced to save the man's life. The man clutched the floatation device as a huge wave knocked both men underwater. The swimmer surfaced. Carlson did not. Searchers recovered his body three hours later.

Every day, at pools and beaches, at ponds and reservoirs, lifeguards face myriad dangers. In most cases, a lifeguard will go from a sitting or standing position to running with all his or her power toward a victim. It can be a jarring, body-numbing experience once they hit the water. As they run, the lifeguard's body is warm, but once submerged, their bodies quickly cool off.

That's just one of the problems lifeguards face. Swimmers might be injured, unconscious, or in many cases, flailing wildly, as they struggle to keep above the waves. The lifeguard has to calm the victim and get him or her out of danger as fast and as safely as possible.

Lifeguards have to battle Mother Nature, too. The bigger the surf, the deeper the rescue worker has to dive under each wave. They do this as they gasp for oxygen. Each year, according to the CDC, 4,000 people die from drowning in the United States.

PROTECT AND SERVE

POLICE OFFICER

Dangers: Shootings, stabbings, car-accident injuries, and other trauma—these are some of the dangers faced by police officers.

Did You Know? Boston established the first police department in 1838.

According to the National Law Enforcement Officers Memorial Fund, between 2008 and 2017, 1,511 police officers died while on duty—that works out to an average of 151 deaths a year. Of that number, 514 were shot to death, 126 were struck by a vehicle, 364 died in automobile crashes, and 325 died as a result of job-related illness. These and other statistics are testament to just how dangerous policing can be.

As far as we know, the first police officer to die in the line of duty occurred in 1791. Since then, about 21,000 law enforcement officers of all stripes have died while on the job in the United States. Cops on the beat have to contend with a variety of situations when they respond to a call. The incident could be as mundane as rescuing a cat stuck in a tree, or as serious as staring down a robber with a pistol. The prospect of death or injury is real. Officers can crash their cars. They can fall or be shot. Danger can come at a traffic stop, during an argument between a husband and wife, or while simply sitting in a patrol car.

That's what happened on July 5, 2018, when New York City police officer Miosotis Familia was gunned down as she sat in a marked police cruiser in the Bronx. It wasn't the first time a police officer was targeted just because he or she wore a badge. On November 29, 2009, an assassin gunned down four members of the Lakewood, Washington, Police Department as they sat in a coffee shop doing paperwork.

The deadliest day in U.S. law enforcement history occurred on September 11, 2001, when 72 law enforcement officers died during the terrorist attacks on New York City and Washington, D.C. Seventy-one officers perished responding to the World Trade Center that day.

A memorial for Officer Miosotis Familia after she was murdered in 2017.

SEARCH-AND-RESCUE WORKER

Dangers: Broken bones, drowning, burning, death.

Did You Know? The U.S. Coast Guard saved 33,000 people during Hurricane Katrina in 2005.

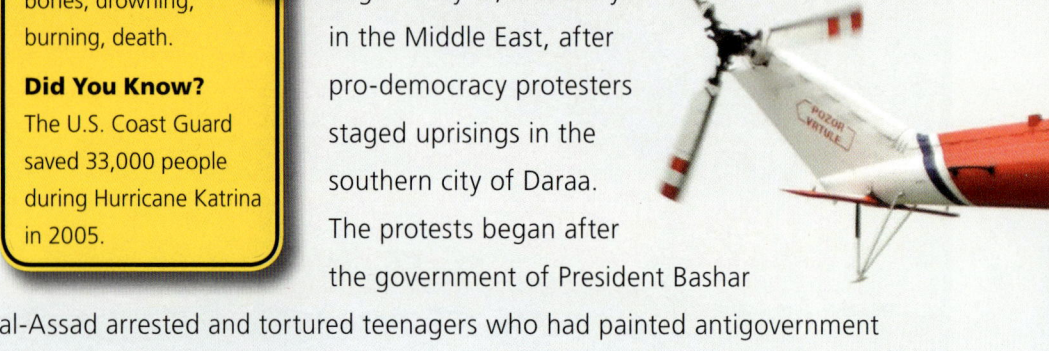

In 2011 a brutal civil war began in Syria, a country in the Middle East, after pro-democracy protesters staged uprisings in the southern city of Daraa. The protests began after the government of President Bashar al-Assad arrested and tortured teenagers who had painted antigovernment slogans on a school wall.

Since that time, tens of thousands of civilians have found themselves in the crosshairs, often trapped in the rubble following air strikes, barrel bombings, and chemical-weapons attacks. When the attacks subside, a group of search-and-rescue workers—the White Helmets—comb through the shattered buildings and streets looking for survivors.

The White Helmets are men and women who volunteer to save lives. Some are bankers, lawyers, tailors, and business owners. All don white helmets so people can tell who they are. Since the start of the war in Syria, the White Helmets have saved more than 100,000 people. Searching for survivors during any type of catastrophe is challenging enough, but to search when bombs are falling and bullets are flying is extremely hazardous. That is why the White Helmets were nominated in 2016 for a Nobel Peace Prize.

Search-and-rescue operations often catch the public's imagination, whether it is a little girl trapped in a well or a group of soccer players trapped in a cave. In many communities, search-and-rescue operations are conducted by police, firefighters, and others. The military also helps in searching and rescuing people, and some private companies have search-and-rescue teams.

ULTIMATE DANGER ULTIMATE DANGER ULTIMATE

A search-and-rescue team demonstrates its skills in the Czech Republic.

MINING FOR MEN

One of the most famous search-and-rescue operations occurred in 2010, when a group of miners in Chile found themselves trapped below ground after a cave-in. Rescuers came from all around the globe. After 69 days, rescue teams pulled the miners from what most assuredly would otherwise have been their tomb. Engineers developed a special torpedo-shaped capsule that they lowered into the ground to pull the trapped men out, one at a time.

SMOKEJUMPER

Dangers: Risks in this profession go from trips and falls to dehydration and death.

Did You Know? Smokejumpers inspired the creation of the U.S. Army's 101st Airborne Division.

In the history of forest fires in the American West, no unit is held in higher regard than the Smokejumpers, an elite Federal crew used as a quick strike squad against the most overpowering of fires. Today, the day after at least 12 firefighters from a crew of 52 were trapped and then killed in a wildfire that "blew up" on a steep slope in Western Colorado, the Smokejumpers are mourning one of their worst disasters in modern times. Two firefighters are still missing.

Smokejumpers over the Channel Islands, California.

THE ULTIMATE BOOK OF DANGEROUS JOBS

So began a frontpage article in the *New York Times* on July 8, 1994. The article describes how 12 firefighters died, as others scrambled to safety. It was one of the worst wildfire disasters in U.S. history.

Smokejumpers are firefighters who parachute out of airplanes to battle stubborn wildfires. First instituted in 1939 in the United States, the elite unit is a part of the U.S. Forest Service and the U.S. Bureau of Land Management. Other countries, most notably Russia, have similar fire brigades.

When they are on a mission, it is the responsibility of a "spotter," a member of the crew, to figure out the best place to jump. Because of their training, the smokejumpers are prepared for any scenario they encounter. Once on the ground, one of the first things a smokejumper must do is to create a "firebreak" to help slow down the encroaching fire. This might include felling trees and clearing dry brush. Often, they'll dig trenches to stop the flames. Smokejumpers are laden with all type of equipment and supplies, including food to last them a few days.

Over the years, approximately 5,000 men and women have served as smokejumpers. Some 30 have died in the line of duty. One of the worst disasters was the 1949 Mann Gulch Fire, which killed 16 smokejumpers as they were trying to move to a safe location.

Watch this video to see smokejumpers in action.

PROTECT AND SERVE

WORDS TO UNDERSTAND

apprentice: trainee
herbicide: weed killer
hydraulic: operated by a liquid under high pressure
regulations: rules enforced by the government, including governing the way industries behave

CHAPTER 3

ON-THE-JOB MAYHEM

If you walk around your neighborhood today, you will probably see a number of different people at work: repairing a roof, fixing a telephone line, cutting grass, or laying a new electrical line to a garage. Although it may not seem like it, all those workers are flirting with injury and even death.

In 2017 the U.S. Bureau of Labor Statistics released a report on the number of fatal work injuries in 2016. At that time, there were a total of 5,190 fatal work injuries recorded in the United States, a 7 percent increase from 2015. It was the third consecutive annual rise in workplace fatalities, and the first time more than 5,000 fatalities had been recorded since 2008. Some were loggers, others were fishermen, and still others were those who pick up your trash. Many were in the construction trades. All were performing services for other people.

Most of us take these jobs for granted, but perhaps we shouldn't. Consider that in 2016, 125 landscapers and groundskeepers died on the job, as did 101 roofers, 84 tree trimmers and pruners, 64 automotive mechanics, and 61 farmers and ranchers. Death doesn't care where you work.

AUTO MECHANIC

Dangers: Trips, falls, cuts, bruises, strained backs and necks, burns—these and more are faced by auto mechanics on the job.

Did You Know? There are nearly 230,000 automotive garages in the United States.

Your family car is making a weird sound. You don't know what it is. You bring it to an automotive repair shop to see what is wrong. A mechanic gives the car the once-over, finds the problem, and then fixes it. The bill might be expensive, but at the end of the day, the car is running as it should.

But garages are hazardous environments in which to work. For one thing, mechanics are around heavy equipment all day, including **hydraulic** car lifts and a number of cumbersome power tools. They must constantly lift heavy items, including mufflers and tires, which can strain backs and necks. Moreover, mechanics spend a lot of time bending down or on their back using tools in awkward positions. While younger mechanics can often weather the strain well, those who are older might find that their bodies don't contort as they once did.

Mechanics are also often exposed to loud noises, which can result in hearing loss. One mistake can cause a mechanic to hurt herself or himself, or another

person. Tools can cut gashes in arms, legs, and hands. Fingers can get smashed by falling auto parts, including tires, mufflers, pipes, and other things. A mechanic can also get burned by battery acid, hot oil, hydraulic fluid, and other liquids. They can also get electrocuted. The fatal injury rate for automotive mechanics in 2016 was 7.2 per 100,000 workers.

ELECTRICIAN

Dangers: Those who work with electricity face various dangers on the job, including trips, falls, cuts, bruises, and strains, as well as the risk of death by electrocution.

Did You Know? There are nearly 700,000 licensed electricians in the United States.

Nathan E. Pruitt was an electrician's **apprentice**, busy learning the trade. It was 2013, and Pruitt was helping remodel a bathroom. As he worked, Pruitt accidently touched a 270 volt electrical line. Electricity ripped through his body, killing him.

Electricity is a curious thing. Modern society can't function without it, and yet electricity is inherently dangerous. It can kill a person instantly. Still, to some extent, electricity can be tamed, and that is the job of electricians who install, maintain, and repair electrical systems.

People who work with electricity can be electrocuted while trying to repair wiring, appliances, light fixtures, air conditioning units, and underground power lines. Yet electrocution is not necessarily the main reason electricians die on the job. In fact, falls are the main source of electrician deaths. Electricians are constantly going up and down ladders or working in high places. They can also get burned from electrical explosions. All it takes is an improper connection, and small particles of metal or copper wire can shoot off in all directions, much like an exploding hand grenade. The fatal injury rate in 2016 was 10 for every 100,000 workers.

Working on high-voltage power lines takes a lot of skill.

ON-THE-JOB MAYHEM

FISHERMAN

Dangers: People who fish for a living face a risk of falls, burns, and drowning.

Did You Know? An old fishing superstition says that sailors who have either tattoos or earrings won't drown.

There's something magical, and perhaps a bit romantic, about fishing on the high seas—the wind spraying saltwater in your face as the boat's nets brim with swordfish, cod, halibut, crab, and other types of seafood. Yet commercial fishing is one of the world's most dangerous occupations.

A case in point is the fishing vessel *Destination*. In 2017 the ship sank in the Bering Sea, just north of St. George, an Alaskan island. The crab boat had sailed out of Seattle, Washington. It was a trip the crew had made dozens of times. The Destination's captain, Jeff Hathaway, was also a seasoned veteran, fishing Alaska's crab grounds for 40 years. Still, regardless of how much experience a fisherman has, deadly situations can arise.

That's what happened on February 10, when an angry sea swallowed the *Destination*. The waters off Alaska are among the most dangerous fishing grounds in the world. In 1993, according to the National Institute for Occupational Safety and Health, 37 commercial fishermen died in Alaskan waters. Over the next 20 years, the numbers fluctuated, but each year, someone dies.

Alaska is not alone. In fact, the Center for Public Integrity reported that "no place . . . is more deadly for commercial fishermen than the East Coast." From 2000 to 2009, 165 commercial fishermen died from Maine to Florida. The reasons they die and are injured are myriad. The leading cause is drowning after a vessel disaster. Others die after falling overboard, while deck injuries constitute the largest number of nonfatal injuries on a fishing boat.

GROUNDS MAINTENANCE WORKER

Dangers: Trips, falls, cuts, bruises, burns, amputations, and possibly death

Did You Know? The U.S. Consumer Product Safety Commission says a typical chainsaw injury requires 110 stitches.

Dewayne Johnson was a school groundskeeper in San Francisco. In addition to mowing the lawn, part of Johnson's job was to kill weeds. As such, he'd fill up a 50 gallon (189 L) tank of **herbicide** and attached it to a truck. He then went about his business spraying the weeds with the poison. He did this for years. Sometimes, when the wind kicked up, the herbicide blew back in his face. Once a hose broke, soaking his body with the poison.

In 2014 Johnson was diagnosed with non-Hodgkin's lymphoma, a form of cancer. He sued the makers of the herbicide, alleging one of its ingredients—glyphosate—made him sick. In the summer of 2018, a jury agreed, awarding him $289 million in damages.

Mowing lawns. Whacking weeds. Pruning shrubs. Planting trees. Chipping logs. Grounds maintenance workers are seemingly all over the place—outside schools and offices, public buildings and parks, sports fields and cemeteries, and in people's yards. But it can be a deadly profession. In 2016 the fatal injury rate was 17.4 per 100,000 full-time workers. According to the CDC, during this five-year period, 15 percent died after being struck by a falling tree or limb; 13 percent were killed after falling from a tree, or were knocked off a ladder by falling branches; 11 percent were killed in highway accidents; and 9 percent died riding lawnmowers or tractors.

Grounds maintenance workers use many different tools and equipment, including chainsaws, mowers, backhoes, and tractors. Accidents can occur at any time. In 2001 a groundskeeper at a Connecticut amusement park was cutting weeds underneath a roller coaster when the coaster smashed into him, splitting his skull open.

CHECK IT OUT!

Walk around your neighborhood at the same time for every day for one week. Chart how many people you see doing utility work, carpentry, roofing, and other jobs mentioned in this chapter. At the end of the five days, create a bar chart showing the number of workers from each occupation. What can you conclude?

ON-THE-JOB MAYHEM

LOGGER

Dangers: Logging can result in trips, falls, amputations, cuts, gashes, or even death.

Did You Know? There are around 55,000 employed loggers in the United States.

As John Garland, a professor at Oregon State University, told British newspaper the *Guardian*, "Logging is difficult, dirty, dangerous, and declining." Death, he continued, "can come from trees falling in the wrong direction or hitting another tree and falling back on someone."

According to the most recent data supplied by U.S. Bureau of Labor Statistics, logging has a fatality rate of 135.9 per 100,000 workers, far outpacing any other occupation. Moreover, 2,449 workers per 100,000 suffer non-life-threating injuries. It's not that hard to figure out why logging is such a lethal business. One mistake, one ill-conceived cut, can send a logger to his death.

Some of the dangers a logger faces comes from the tools being used. Not only do loggers use chainsaws, but they are also schooled in how to use several types of heavy machinery. The environment in which loggers work can add to the danger. Loggers often work in remote forests, cutting down and removing trees from high atop cliffs and mountainsides. These job sites are often far from medical help. In addition, bad weather, which can turn a dry hillside into mud, can make the job site as slick as an ice rink. Logs can slip and fall; trucks can overturn. A logger can lose his or her grip on a chainsaw, steel cables, or other equipment. All these factors add to the risk.

Logging on Vancouver Island, Canada.

MINER

Inside a gold mine in Russia.

Dangers: Cave-ins and explosions can result in death, dismemberment, and various illnesses.

Did You Know? Today, Chinese mines are the world's most deadly. Official government numbers report the death of an average of 2 miners per day, but another estimate suggests the real number could be as high as 13 miners killed per day.

Chapter 2 related the story of a group of Chilean miners who had to be rescued from what was very nearly an underground tomb. They were lucky: they all survived. Yet over the decades, mine disasters have taken their toll. Whether it is a coal mine, a copper mine, or a gold mine, those who extract these and other materials from the earth live a dangerous existence.

Cave-ins, explosions, and equipment accidents are just some of the hazards miners face. Luckily, new safety laws and procedures have spared thousands of lives in recent years. Consider that in the United States, an average of 1,500 mining deaths of all types occurred each year prior to the 1990s. Since safety **regulations** were enacted, the fatality rate dropped significantly: there were 15 miners killed in coal mines in 2017, and 13 deaths in other types of mining operations.

Although safety procedures have reduced the chances of death and injury, miners still face a variety of hazards, including health risks that can crop up later. Miners who work underground are at risk of developing respiratory issues caused by inadequate ventilation systems. They are also exposed to variety of hazardous substances, including radon, a natural, odorless radioactive gas that can lead to lung cancer. Breathing in dust is a major issue, too. Blasting and drilling creates fine dust particles that can accumulate and damage lungs, a condition called *pneumoconiosis*.

ROOFER

Dangers: Falling off roofs and ladders can result in serious injury, as can the improper use of tools.

Did You Know? Nail guns shoot nails under high pressure—around 120 pounds per square inch.

Roofers are the high-flying acrobats of the building trades, precariously scampering over steep inclines as they lay shingles and make sure that everyone has a solid roof over their head.

How dangerous is roofing? According to the U.S. government, 101 roofers died on the job in 2016. That number translates into 49 deaths per 100,000 workers. Moreover, roofers sustained 3,150 nonfatal injuries. The most common hazards are falls. Falls from the edges of roofs account for nearly 90 percent of roofer fall-deaths. According to the U.S. Bureau of Labor Statistics, roofing is America's fifth most dangerous job.

Laying down a roof is not easy. It involves heavy lifting, climbing, bending, and kneeling. Most of these activities take place on rooftops, scaffolds, and ladders. Roofers work with potentially dangerous tools, including nail guns, hoists, electric drills, circular saws, and other power equipment. Injuries, such as cuts and amputations, can occur when these tools are not used properly.

Falling debris can also cause injuries. Electrocution is another danger. Roofers often work close to power lines. Climbing a metal ladder can be deadly if a worker places it next to a power line.

STEEL AND IRON WORKER

Dangers: Falls, burns, and other traumas are possible.

Did You Know? Around 200 members of the Mohawk Indian Tribe work as steelworkers in New York City.

Christopher Gunn was 28, a steelworker who helped keep New York City's skyline reaching toward the clouds. In April 2008 Gunn was working on a building under construction on East 29th Street in Manhattan. He was trying to maneuver a 20-foot steel beam into its proper place. At around 8:30 a.m., Gunn slipped and fell from the building's second story, slamming his body into a concrete slab. He survived, but just barely.

Inspectors said Gunn was wearing his required safety gear, including a harness. However, the harness was not tied to any object that would have prevented him from falling; under federal rules, Gunn was not required to secure the harness's safety strap if he was working at a height no higher than 30 feet.

Regardless, the fall illustrates the perils that ironworkers and steelworkers face every day. Whether they are climbing tall structures or working with superhot welding equipment, the fatality rate in 2016 for steelworkers was 25.1 deaths per 100,000 full-time workers. Falling from tremendous heights is just one of the dangers. Surfaces often get slick because of ice, snow, or rain. One misstep, and a person can tumble to his or her death.

Cuts, abrasions, and muscle strains are also common, because working on such structures taxes the body. Burns from welding equipment can scorch faces, hands, legs, and torsos, and sparks can fly into the eyes if proper safety equipment is not worn.

Building a new skyscraper in New York City's financial district, 2018.

ON-THE-JOB MAYHEM

UTILITY WORKER

Dangers: Utility workers risk falls, burns, and death from explosions or noxious fumes.

Did You Know? The voltage of electricity moving across long-distance electrical transmission lines ranges between 155,000 and 765,000 volts.

Elway Gray was walking down a street in Key Largo, Florida, in 2017 when he noticed that a section of the newly paved road was not settling properly. Gray, 34 years old at the time, was a utility worker charged with making sure power was flowing to a nearby subdivision. He decided to see what the problem was. He took off the manhole cover and descended into the earth under the road. He didn't come up, nor did he answer calls from his coworkers. Troubled by the silence, Louis O' Keefe and Robert Wilson descended into the street to see if their colleague was okay. Neither knew what was waiting for them. All three died, overcome by noxious fumes.

Several months later, the U.S. Labor Department's Occupational Safety and Health Administration (OSHA) blamed the workers' employer for the deaths. Officials cited the company for not ventilating the manhole before the men went in to investigate. As a result, all three were overcome by lethal levels of hydrogen sulfide and carbon monoxide, both poisonous gases. OSHA also blamed the company for inadequate training and the lack of on-site equipment that could have detected the hazardous gases.

"The hazards of working in manholes are well established, but there are ways to make it safe," OSHA's director in Fort Lauderdale said in a statement, after slapping the company with $100,000 in fines. "Three employees needlessly lost their lives and others were injured due to their employer's failure to follow safe work practices."

Utility workers have one of the highest death and injury rates in the construction trades. Around 30 to 50 workers die each year on the job for every 100,000 workers. Utility workers come in all stripes. Some make sure that homes

Utility work in Bangkok, Thailand.

and businesses have gas and power. Others make sure the phones work, while others tend to cable and Internet service.

All risk electrical shock and electrocution. They are also at risk from falls from basket cranes, utility poles, and ladders. Gas workers are always concerned about being exposed to toxic gas. They fear explosions every time they dig up a gas line or check homes and buildings. These are only some of the hazards that utility workers face. They can also trip and fall in a customer's backyard or at a power substation. In addition, they often work along roadsides, making them vulnerable to passing cars or trucks.

WASTE COLLECTOR AND HAULER

Dangers: Waste collectors risk being crushed, poisoned, infected, or struck by vehicles.

Did You Know? Americans generate 254 million tons of trash each year.

Waste haulers are a common sight in cities and towns. It would seem, at least on its face, that collecting trash isn't a very dangerous occupation. But in reality, garbage collectors are often taking their lives into their own hands.

For one thing, garbage collectors never know what is hiding in a trash or recycling bin. People throw out all sorts of stuff, from battery acid to bleach, from pesticides and herbicides to hypodermic needles. Occasionally, people unwittingly discard radioactive material—for example, if a sick person undergoes radiation therapy, the patient's radioactive body fluids, such as mucus, can contaminate tissues and other products.

Workers handling toxic waste in California.

Trash haulers can be poisoned, burned, or infected with a dangerous pathogen. In addition to the risks posed by hazardous materials, trash collectors also work with big machines

Watch this video to see a day in the life of a garbage collector.

that can crush anyone and anything. Physical injuries can occur when lifting heavy bags or containers of trash and recyclables. Workers can also fall during bad weather, or be struck by oncoming vehicles. In 2017 there were 35 deaths for every 100,000 full-time workers.

WORDS TO UNDERSTAND

allied: joined as part of an alliance
booby traps: seemingly harmless objects that contain an explosive device designed to kill or maim
ford: to cross a river
reconnaissance: military observation of a specific area to locate an enemy or to figure out the region's strategic features

THE ULTIMATE BOOK OF DANGEROUS JOBS

CHAPTER 4

IN SERVICE TO COUNTRY

Every day, in every nation, men and women risk their lives because they love their country. Some are soldiers dressed in uniforms. They ride in tanks, or parachute into enemy territory. They help people in times of need. Others are fighter pilots. Some serve in elite special operations units. Still others work as spies.

There are many reasons why people aspire to this line of work. Some serve out of a sense of duty. Others use their service as a pathway for economic and social mobility. What's more, they can use the skills they learn in service of their country later in life. These are not easy jobs by any stretch. Those who serve must learn to follow orders and work as a team.

In this chapter, you will read about some of the more dangerous jobs that people do in service to their country.

COMBAT ENGINEER

Dangers: Serious injury and death are possible, not only from the enemy, but from clearing landmines or working with heavy machinery and other equipment.

Did You Know? One of the greatest combat engineering feats in history was Napoleon's retreat from Moscow, which would never have happened without a hastily built pontoon bridge.

Building things, such as roads and bridges, is always dangerous, even under the best of conditions. But imagine trying to accomplish such a task in a war zone, with bombs raining down on you, or snipers taking aim at you. It is all in a day's work for combat engineers.

When the infantry is bogged down because they cannot **ford** a river, or because they cannot remove a mountain of obstacles, they'll call the engineers for help. Every military around the world uses combat engineers. They work as a team to accomplish certain tasks, such as building roads and bridges, constructing combat positions, removing explosives, and building landing zones for helicopters. They are also tasked with removing **booby traps** and camouflaging tanks and other equipment, so the enemy cannot see them.

Combat engineers often find themselves in the middle of the fight. They'll use bulldozers while being shot at. They'll direct bomb disposal robots to disarm improvised explosive devices (IEDs). The list of things they can do under the most stressful situations is extraordinary.

Find out more about the treacherous job of combat engineer.

HURRICANE HUNTER

Dangers: Crashes and airplane failures often result in death.

Did You Know? Hurricane Hunters don't carry parachutes.

A WC-130J Hurricane Hunter aircraft over the Georgia coast.

When a hurricane is blowing across the open water and taking aim at land, a group of men and women fly into the storm to gather as much information as possible. They are known as the Hurricane Hunters. Specifically, they are members of the 53rd Weather Reconnaissance Squadron, part of the Air Force's 403rd Reserve Wing. (Other hurricane hunters work for the National Oceanic and Atmospheric Administration [NOAA].)

The average mission lasts about 11 hours. Each mission is made up of 6 to 15 people, including the flight crew and the scientific crew. Their main job is to locate the center of the storm and determine the maximum wind speed. They will tell the flight crew where to steer the aircraft. They'll also conduct various experiments.

The crew will then send the information they gleaned via satellite to NOAA, where scientists can analyze it and make a forecast. Government authorities can then use that information to keep people safe. Several Air Force Hurricane Hunter airplanes have gone down—in 1952, 1958, and 1974. One Navy plane was lost in 1952. All told, 36 Hurricane Hunters and their passengers have died.

PARARESCUE JUMPER

Dangers: Death and injuries, especially in combat situations

Did You Know? Airman First Class William H. Pitsenbarger was the first pararescue jumper to win the Congressional Medal of Honor.

When soldiers are injured on the battlefield, a group of airmen swoop in, scoop them up, and get them out of harm's way. They are members of the pararescue force: the military's ambulance service. Pararescue jumpers (PJs) are among the most elite troops in the U.S. military. More than 3,200 have served in the unit since the end of World War II. Today, only 500 airmen are part of the force, serving alongside other military units and **allied** soldiers.

PJs provide soldiers and civilians with urgent medical care. They are also trained to fight in small units. They can parachute into remote locations with their equipment from both high and low altitudes. They are often called in to rescue people from buildings that have collapsed or from vehicle wrecks. Over the decades the PJs have gotten into some gnarly situations, which is why they are the most decorated U.S. Air Force unit. Their motto is "These Things We Do, That Others May Live."

It's not easy to become a PJ. It takes two years of intense physical and mental training. Each PJ must learn how to deal with extreme environments, such as working in cold or extremely hot conditions. They must master jumping out of airplanes and helicopters at night. They go to diving school and are well-versed in saving lives on the battlefield. Ninety percent of all PJ recruits wash out, or drop out, of the program.

Pararescue teams have been used in more than 35,000 combat or humanitarian missions over the years. In 1966 they helped rescue two U.S. astronauts, Neil Armstrong and David Scott, after their Gemini space capsule made an emergency splashdown. Pararescue teams also tended to the injured stuck under a collapsed highway following a deadly 1989 earthquake in San Francisco.

One of their greatest triumphs occurred in Afghanistan in February 2010. At that time, the PJs evacuated more than 300 Afghans who had become stranded

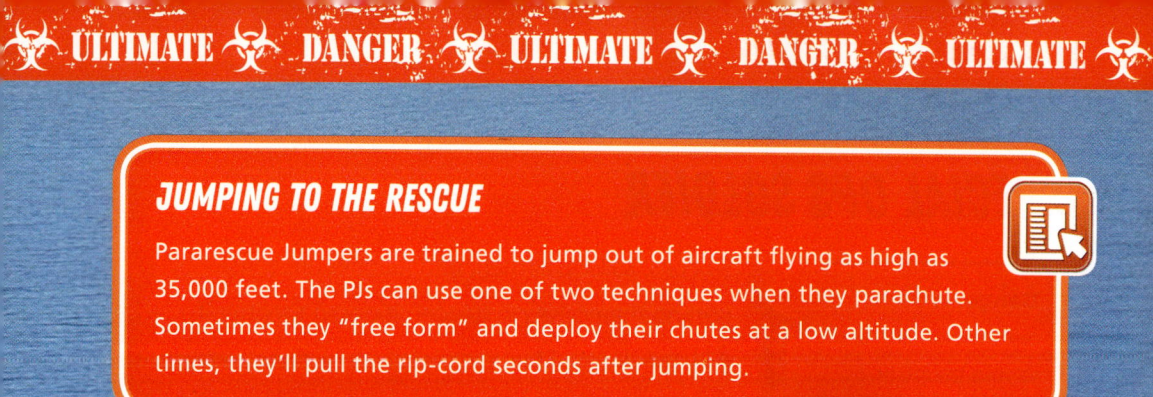

JUMPING TO THE RESCUE

Pararescue Jumpers are trained to jump out of aircraft flying as high as 35,000 feet. The PJs can use one of two techniques when they parachute. Sometimes they "free form" and deploy their chutes at a low altitude. Other times, they'll pull the rip-cord seconds after jumping.

Pararescue jumpers with the Air Force's 304th Expeditionary Rescue Squadron, Djibouti, in Africa.

after a series of avalanches brought down tons of snow on their homes. At times the temperature dipped to 40 degrees below zero. Battling snow, high winds, and bone-numbing temperatures, the PJs responded to the catastrophe in helicopters. It wasn't easy. The PJs had to work in brutal cold, at an elevation of nearly 12,000 feet (3657.6 m), while constantly under threat from enemy forces. Their training was put to good use, and they got all the survivors out.

SPECIAL OPS SOLDIER

Dangers: Death, dismemberment, and various traumatic injuries are possible.

Did You Know?
One of the first special ops units was Ethan Allen and his Green Mountain Boys during the American Revolution (1775–1783).

Soldiers, sailors, airmen, and marines are constantly putting themselves in danger. It doesn't matter if they are deployed in a war zone or working to bring food and medicine to those in need. They work with dangerous weapons and potentially lethal machinery. Soldiering, whether on the high seas, in the desert, or in the jungle, is a physically and mentally demanding job.

One of the toughest assignments is serving in combat units, including special operations, or special ops, forces. Special ops units accomplish remarkable

Navy SEALs crossing a river.

things. For example, a special operations unit killed Osama bin Laden, the mastermind of the 2001 terrorist attacks on Washington, D.C., and New York City.

Many times, the public will not hear about their exploits until long after the soldiers have returned home—and sometimes not at all. Nearly all nations have these special elite units. They fight in combat and conduct rescue missions. They are often used to kidnap or kill suspected terrorists or enemy soldiers. They battle pirates on the ocean and bring criminals to justice.

The iconic moment when President Obama and his security team watched live as a special ops team captured and killed Osama Bin Laden.

Special ops units in the United States include the Navy SEALs, Army Green Berets, and Army Rangers, among others. The training is both physically demanding and mentally exhausting. They must learn to use a variety of weapons and equipment. They must know how to tend to the wounded and become experts in demolition and **reconnaissance**. In the last few years, U.S. special operations troops have died in greater numbers than regular, or conventional, troops. When the wars in Iraq and Afghanistan were at their peak, special ops units made up only a tiny fraction of those killed in battle. Not anymore. The Pentagon has come to depend on these elite warriors to get the job done.

CHECK IT OUT!

Research the history of one U.S. special ops forces mentioned here. Use the library and Internet. Next, create a computer slideshow showing the group's achievements and missions.

IN SERVICE TO COUNTRY

SERIES GLOSSARY OF KEY TERMS

anaphylaxis: a type of severe and potentially fatal allergic reaction

antibiotic: any of a class of drugs that can inhibit or destroy microorganisms that cause illness

arid: having little or no rain

asphyxiation: to deprive one of air; to choke or suffocate an animal to death

benign: not harmful

blunt-force trauma: an injury caused by colliding with something

bona fide: genuine, real

booby traps: seemingly harmless objects that contain an explosive device designed to kill or maim

camouflage: a defense mechanism animals use to blend into their surroundings to escape predators

cannibalism: the practice of eating the flesh of one's own species

cartel: an association of suppliers

class action: a type of lawsuit filed on behalf of a large group or "class" of people

claustrophobic: extremely fearful of confined places

climate change: a change in global or regional climate patterns attributed largely to the effects of greenhouse gases, such as carbon dioxide

cyanide: an extremely toxic chemical compound

deforestation: the destruction of forests by humans

degenerative: wasting away

demilitarized zone: an area between warring countries that is devoid of military installations, based on treaties or other agreements

destitute: extremely poor

disoriented: confused

emaciated: dangerously thin, due to lack of food

endurance: able to withstand something difficult

entomologist: a scientist who studies insects

envenomate: the process by which venom is injected by means of a bite or sting

exploited: taken advantage of

extrajudicial: beyond or outside the legal system

fire suppressant: a chemical that can extinguish a fire

flotsam: bits and pieces of debris floating on the water

frostbite: injury caused to body tissue by exposure to extreme cold

genotoxic: describes something that can cause genetic mutations

gore: to stab with a horn or tusk

hypothermia: abnormally low body temperature

insurgency: rebellion

inundated: flooded, swamped

malaria: a serious and sometimes fatal infectious disease that is spread by certain types of mosquitoes

ordnance: military explosives, such as missiles and bombs

pathogen: bacterium, virus, or microorganism that can cause disease

perilous: dangerous

pheromone: a chemical substance produced and released into the environment by an organism, which affects the behavior of others in its species

predators: animals that prey on others

regulations: rules enforced by the government, including governing the way industries behave

sinkhole: an opening in the ground caused by a variety of factors, including erosion

squeamish: easily nauseated or disgusted

stamina: the ability to withstand continued physical activity

torrential: relentless rain

treacherous: extremely risky

venerate: worship

vernacular: everyday language

SERIES GLOSSARY OF KEY TERMS

FURTHER READING AND INTERNET RESOURCES

BOOKS

Corwin, Marshall. *Extreme Survival: An Adventurer's Guide to the World's Most Dangerous Places.* New York: Skyhorse, 2010.

Dangerous Jobs in Action. Book Series. North Mankato, MN: The Child's World, 2017.

Emergency! Book Series. North Mankato, MN: Capstone, 2016.

Perritano, John. *Bomb Squad Technician.* On a Mission. Broomall, PA: Mason Crest, 2015.

Pushies, Fred. *U.S. Special Ops: The History, Weapons, and Missions of Elite Military Forces.* Minneapolis, MN: Quarto USA, 2016.

Smylie, Mike. *The Perilous Catch: A History of Commercial Fishing.* History's Most Dangerous Jobs. Stroud, UK: The History Press, 2015.

Walker, Brad. *The Anatomy of Sports Injuries: Your Guide to Prevention, Diagnosis, and Treatment.* Berkeley, CA: North Atlantic Books, 2018.

WEBSITES

Forbes: "Inside the Life of a Rodeo Clown"
https://www.forbes.com/2009/05/05/rodeo-clown-inside-lifestyle-sports-rodeo-clown.html#5a97d1434ea6
A good article about rodeo clowns, including a short history.

Global Forest Atlas

> https://globalforestatlas.yale.edu/forest-use-logging/logging
>
> You can find tons of information about logging and forest use on this website, presented by the Yale School of Forestry & Environmental Studies.

National Oceanographic and Atmospheric Administration: "Hurricane Hunters"

> https://oceantoday.noaa.gov/hurricanehunters
>
> A cool video and transcript describing the job of NOAA's Hurricane Hunters.

Space.com: "Gravity and Reality"

> https://www.space.com/23182-gravity-film-worst-space-disasters.html
>
> Check out this site if you are interested in the world's worst space disasters.

VIDEO CLIPS

CHAPTER 1

Watch this video and see how Chris Gillette "wrestles" an alligator.

> http://x-qr.net/1K8d

CHAPTER 2

Watch this video to see smokejumpers in action.

> http://x-qr.net/1KSV

CHAPTER 3

Watch this video to see a day in the life of a garbage collector.

> http://x-qr.net/1M1z

CHAPTER 4

Find out more about the treacherous job of combat engineer.

> http://x-qr.net/1Jky

INDEX

acrobats, 18
Ali, Muhammad, 14, 15
Allen, Ethan, 70
alligator wrestlers, 10–11
Apollo I, 32
Arnaud, Yann, 18
astronauts, 32–33
athletics
    alligator wrestlers, 10–11
    background, 9
    baseball players, 12–13
    boxers, 14–15
    bullfighters, 22–23
    football players, 16–17
    gymnasts, 18
    hockey players, 19
    jockeys, 20
    race car drivers, 8, 24–25
    rugby players, 27
    See also jobs of protection and
        service; military; performers;
        trade industries
auto mechanics, 50

baseball players, 12–13
Beatty, Clyde, 21
bombs and bomb threats, 34, 40
bomb squad technicians, 34–35
boxers, 14–15
Bugrimova, Irina, 21
bullfighters, 22–23

Carlson, Ben, 41
Chaffee, Roger, 32
Challenger (space shuttle), 33
Cobb, Ty, 12
combat engineers, 66
Conigliaro, Tony, 12–13
cosmonauts, 32

dangers to
    acrobats, 18
    astronauts, 32–33
    auto mechanics, 50
    baseball players, 12–13
    bomb squad technicians, 34
    bullfighters, 22, 23
    combat engineers, 66
    electricians, 51
    emergency medical technicians, 36
    epidemiologists, 37
    firefighters, 38–39
    fishermen, 52–53
    football players, 16, 17
    groundskeepers, 54
    gymnasts, 18
    hockey players, 19
    Hurricane Hunters, 67
    jockeys, 20
    landmine removers, 40
    lifeguards, 41
    lion tamers, 21

loggers, 56
miners, 45, 57
paramedics, 36
pararescue jumpers, 68
police officers, 42
race car drivers, 24–25
rodeo clowns, 26
roofers, 58
rugby players, 27
search and rescue workers, 44
smokejumpers, 46, 47
snake charmers, 28
snake milkers, 29
special operations soldiers, 70
utility workers, 60–61
waste haulers, 62–63
Destination (ship), 52

Earnhardt, Dale, Sr., 24
Ebola, 37
Edwards, Carl, 25
Edwards, Turk, 16
electricians and electricity, 51, 60
emergency medical technicians (EMTs), 36
epidemiologists, 37

Fajfrowski, Louis, 27
Familia, Miosotis, 42–43
Fandiño, Iván, 23
fatality rates
    of astronauts, 32
    of auto mechanics, 50
    of boxers, 14–15
    from drowning, 41
    of electricians, 51
    of emergency medical technicians, 36
    of firefighters, 39
    of fishermen, 52–53
    of groundskeepers, 54
    of Hurricane Hunters, 67
    from landmines, 40
    of loggers, 56
    of miners, 57
    of police officers, 42
    of race car drivers, 25
    of roofers, 58
    of rugby players, 27
    of steelworkers, 59
    of utility workers, 60
    of waste haulers, 63
Fawkes, Guy, 34
firefighters, 30, 38–39, 46–47
fishermen, 52–53
Flores, Jose, 20
football players, 16–17

Gillette, Chris, 10–11
Grandcamp (ship), 38
Gray, Elway, 60
Grissom, Gus, 32
groundskeepers, 54–55
Gunn, Christopher, 59
gymnasts, 18

Hamilton, Jack, 12
Hathaway, Jeff, 52
hockey players, 19
Hughes, Charles Frederick (Chuck), 16

Hurricane Hunters, 67

improvised explosive devices (IEDs), 34, 66
injury rates to
    athletes, 9
    baseball players, 13
    emergency medical technicians, 36
    football players, 17
    hockey players, 19
    jockeys, 20
    rugby players, 27
ironworkers, 59

jobs of protection and service
    astronauts, 32–33
    background, 31
    bomb squad technicians, 34–35
    emergency medical technicians, 36
    epidemiologists, 37
    firefighters, 30, 38–39, 46–47
    landmine removers, 40
    lifeguards, 41
    paramedics, 36
    police officers, 42–43
    search and rescue workers, 44–45
    smokejumpers, 46–47
    See also athletics; military; performers; trade industries
jockeys, 20
Johnson, Dewayne, 54
Johnson, Rashad, 16

Kim, Duk-koo, 14
Knyvett, Thomas, 34

landmine removers, 40
Lane-Claypon, Janet Elizabeth, 37
lifeguards, 41
lion tamers, 21
loggers, 56

Malarchuk, Cline, 19
Mancini, Ray (Boom Boom), 14
Mann Gulch Fire, 47
Martin, Henri, 21
matadors, 22–23
McAuliffe, Christa, 33
McCandless, Bruce, 33
Miccosukee tribes, 10
military
    background, 64–65
    combat engineers, 66
    Hurricane Hunters, 67
    pararescue jumpers, 68–69
    special operations soldiers, 70–71
    See also athletics; jobs of protection and service; performers; trade industries
miners, 45, 57
Mohawk tribes, 59

Native Americans, 10, 59

paramedics, 36
pararescue jumpers, 68–69
performers
    acrobats, 18
    lion tamers, 21
    rodeo clowns, 26

snakes and snake handlers, 28, 29
    See also athletics; jobs of protection and service; military; trade industries
picadors, 22
Plante, Jacques, 19
police officers, 42–43
Pruitt, Nathan E., 51

race car drivers, 8, 24–25
Reagan, Ronald, 41
rodeo clowns, 26
Romero, Francisco, 22
roofers, 58
rugby players, 27

safety equipment
    for epidemiologists, 37
    for race car drivers, 24
    for steelworkers, 59
    for utility workers, 60
search and rescue workers, 44–45
Seminole tribes, 10
September 11, 2001 attacks, 39, 42
Shaheen, Islam, 21
ship disasters, 38, 52
smokejumpers, 46–47
snake charmers, 28
snake milkers, 29
Sosnitskaya, Alla, 18
space program disasters, 32, 33
special operations soldiers, 70–71
steelworkers, 59

Taylor, Lawrence, 16
Tereshkova, Valentina, 32
Theismann, Joe, 16
trade industries
    auto mechanics, 50
    background, 48–49
    electricians, 51
    fishermen, 52–53
    groundskeepers, 54–55
    ironworkers, 59
    loggers, 56
    miners, 45, 57
    roofers, 58
    steelworkers, 59
    utility workers, 60–61
    waste haulers, 62–63
    See also athletics; jobs of protection and service; military; performers
training
    for bomb squad technicians, 34–35
    for pararescue jumpers, 68
    for special operations soldiers, 71
trash collectors, 62–63
Tyson, Mike, 14

utility workers, 60–61

waste haulers, 62–63
Wheldon, Dan, 25
White, Edward, II, 32
White Helmets, 44
Williams, Jerome, 13

AUTHOR'S BIOGRAPHY

John Perritano is an award-winning journalist and author of many nonfiction books for children, including many on science. He holds a master's degree in U.S. history from Western Connecticut State University. He is a former editor at Scholastic and has written a number of books and articles for publishers such as Mason Crest, Time/Life, Time For Kids, Discovery.com, Howstuffworks.com, *Popular Mechanics*, and *National Geographic*.

PHOTO CREDITS

Cover
Shutterstock: main, Gorodenkoff
Dreamstime: lower left, ID 52095665 © Steve Mann; lower center, 73346845 © Oleg Zabielin; lower right, ID 61666916 © FlyingRussiany

Repeating Graphics
Shutterstock: banner, Vector Images; danger symbol, iunewind

Interior
Dreamstime: 1, ID 28560419 © Jpldesigns; 7, ID 68074697 © CarolRobert; 8, ID 13545107 © Walter Arce; 11, ID 39926396 © Fabio Formaggio; 15, ID 50023957 © Jerry Coli; 17, ID 35440082 © Paul Topp; 18, ID 113458790 © Fmua; 19, ID 23020487 © Jerry Coli; 20, ID 455711 © Miltudog; 22-23, ID 92539419 © Nikolai Sorokin; 25, ID 9133492 © Walter Arce; 27, ID 73950313 © Stef22; 28, ID 18289890 © Danielal; 29, ID 71580541 © Leblond Catherine; 30, ID 100412419 © Burnstuff2003; 36, ID 83520377 © blurf; 39, ID 46794609 © Burnstuff2003; 40, ID 24228552 © Amanda Lewis; 41, ID 98888346 © Diana Gradeva; 43, ID 95939974 © Eddie Toro; 44-45, ID 19813274 © Hamik; 48, ID 44971618 © Hoxuanhuong; 50, ID 41305532 © Mirko Vitali; 51, ID 120178059 © Michael Turner; 52-53, ID 61666916 © Flyingrussian; 55, ID 28710545 © Robert Luca; 56, ID 108990272 © Roxana Gonzalez; 57, ID 65811687 © Mark Agnor; 58, ID 32317189 © Racorn; 59, ID 121565107 © Jjfarq; 61,, ID 128057401 © Tuayai; 62-63,, ID 26257937 © Joe Sohm; 64, ID 17870417 © Alberto Dubini
Shutterstock: 21 Sergey Petrov; 37, Chaikom; 70, Get Military Photos
Wikimedia: 13, Keith Allison; 26, US Customs and Border Protection; 32, NASA; 35 Chris Fletcher/MOD; 46, Santa Cruz Jump/Pacific Southwest Region 5; 67, United States Air Force/Tech. Sgt. James Pritchett; 69, U.S. Navy photo by Photographer's Mate 2nd Class Roger S. Duncan; 71, Pete Souza/White House